# HOW TO USE THIS BOOK

PowerWords™ SAT® Verbal Prep Series was designed as a new program to help you learn the 1000 "Must-Know" SAT vocabulary words...without memorizing!

The key ingredient in the design and development of PowerWords™ is humor. Through the innovative use of clever sentences, funny cartoons, and a technique called "Visual Imaging," the meaning of the target word and its picture are permanently imprinted in your memory. Not only have we created cartoons for some of our favorite words, but we have also asked you to create some of your own. Don't be intimidated — the concept of the word which you concretize in your drawing is what's important, not your artistic talent. THE VALUE OF THIS APPROACH CANNOT BE OVERESTIMATED. All of the latest research on memory and cognition affirms the fact that the best way to enhance recall of vocabulary is to create a visual picture in your mind's eye. When you draw your own cartoon, you are doing just this!

Each workbook teaches 400 SAT words. Every target word is followed by:
  • an easy definition (*in italic*) ... this is not an SAT word.
  • 3 or 4 SAT synonyms (***in bold italic***)
  • a clever, witty sentence which presents the word in context.

Although 100 target words are presented, upon completion of each book you will have learned 400 SAT words. All lessons include challenging reinforcement exercises, which are carefully devised to lead you further away from concrete knowledge and rote memorization, to a more subtle awareness of language and the place of words in it. At the end of each book there is a PowerWords™ SAT® THESAURUS. It is alphabetized and cross-referenced to provide easy access to all of the SAT words and their synonyms. The more you use it, the more quickly the words will become a familiar part of your living vocabulary.

So relax, kick back, and let yourself become involved in the wordplay of PowerWords™. Watch your verbal power grow and your SAT score potential rise. But mainly, be aware that the evolution of your verbal mastery helps put **you** in control. *Discover the power of words!*

# TABLE OF CONTENTS

# LESSON 1

Welcome to a new world of words. Wait! Don't panic. Assuage your fears ...you'll enjoy it! Lesson 1 sets the stage for all the lessons to follow. The vocabulary uses fun sentences: some are terse, some are not; some rhyme, others don't — most are pretty goofy. And the cartoons will indelibly imprint the words in your mind. Some are drawn for you, others you'll draw yourself (talent doesn't count — stick figures will do just fine). Mainly, this plethora of SAT words will not be evanescent. The challenge begins now, with the MYSTERY WORD below the cartoon. Just follow all the directions, and with wanton abandon, let yourself meander through Lesson 1.

**Fill in the mystery word when you come to the sentence about the celebrity.**

**The celebrity moved with _____ to escape the autograph hounds.**

# VOCABULARY

1.  **acerbic** (uh ser' bik) adj.

    *bitter, sour, tart, acerbate, pungent, caustic*

    The lemon's **acerbic**, bitter taste
    made Mim's mouth pucker in distaste.

2.  **celerity** (seh leh' rih tee) n.

    *speed, velocity, dispatch, legerity*

    The celebrity moved with **celerity** to escape the autograph hounds.

3.  **choleric** (koh layr' ik) adj.

    *grouchy, sour, irascible, querulous, bilious*

    Carl's **choleric** boss was constantly cranky and cantankerous.

4.  **disparage** (dis paa' rij) v.

    *to degrade, discredit, asperse, malign, calumniate*

    Gossip columnists will **disparage** and defame,
    to get the poop for a scoop on any hot name.

5.  **divine** (dih vine') v.

    *to predict, intuit, augur*

    "A penny for your thoughts," was a saying at one time;
    but to **divine** your thoughts today, would cost more than a dime!.

**DIRECTIONS:** Draw a cartoon to illustrate the word beneath each box.
(Stick figures will work just fine.)

| | | |
|---|---|---|
| | | |
| **divine** | **choleric** | **acerbic** |

6. **exigent** (eggs' ih jint) adj.

   *critical, **crucial, pivotal, importunate***

   Access to the exit is **exigent** in an emergency.

7. **extricate** (ex' trih kate) v.

   *to free, **disembroil, disentwine, disengage***

   It's tricky to **extricate** yourself from a sticky situation.

8. **fecund** (feh' kuhnd) adj.

   *productive, **fertile, fruitful, fructiferous***

   I'll get good crops, the farmer reckoned,
   'cause this here land is so fertile and **fecund**.

9. **germane** (jer mane') adj.

   *appropriate, **relevant, pertinent, apposite, apropos***

   Whether it's germs, Germans, or gerbils,
   all facts must pertain and be **germane**.

10. **indelible** (in del' lih bul) adj.

    *permanent, **immutable, irrevocable, irreparable***

    The fender bender made an **indelible** dent in Troy's Toyota.

## DIRECTIONS: Draw a cartoon to illustrate the word beneath each box.

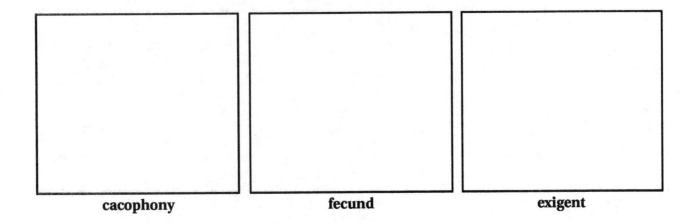

| cacophony | fecund | exigent |

11. **mandatory** (man'dah tor ee) adj.

    *required, obligatory, prescriptive*

    Commanders' mandates are **mandatory**; so obey what they say.

12. **paucity** (paw' cih tee) n.

    *shortage, scarcity, sparsity, dearth*

    The barber said, with a knowledgeable air,
    "Baldness, my friends, is a **paucity** of hair."

13. **regal** (ree' gul) adj.

    *royal, king-like, imperial, majesterial, sovereign*

    The king of the birds is the **regal** eagle.

14. **ribald** (rih' buhld) adj.

    *vulgar, coarse, obscene, irreverent, scurrilous*

    On T.V., the comic was funny and clean,
    but his nightclub act was **ribald** and obscene.

15. **shyster** (shy' stur) n.

    *swindler, quack, defrauder, trickster*

    The sly shyster's shady shenanigans
    landed him in jail without any bail.

## DIRECTIONS: Draw a cartoon to illustrate the word beneath each box.

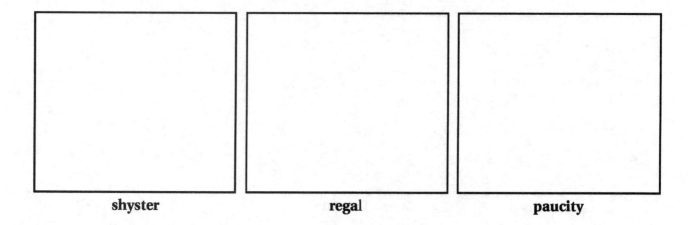

| shyster | regal | paucity |

16. **spurious** (spyour' ee us) adj.

    *counterfeit, simulated, supposititious, ersatz*

    He was bewildered, but she was furious,

    when the jeweler informed them that the diamond was **spurious**.

17. **stalemate** (stale' mate) n.

    *a standstill, impasse, deadlock, a draw*

    "Come on mate - it's getting late!

    Lets' call it a draw and end this **stalemate**."

18. **tawdry** (taw' dree) adj.

    *gaudy, shameless, garish, flagrant, brazen*

    With her unrefined manners and terrible taste,

    she was called "**Tawdry** Audrey" right to her face.

19. **transgress** (tranz gress') v.

    *to trespass, to sin, overstep, encroach, impinge*

    It was clear from her sexy, sultry dress,

    that Delilah intended for Samson to **transgress**.

20. **wanderlust** (wahn' der lust) n.

    *desire to travel, desire to peregrinate, to roam, or to rove*

    Wanda's lust for travel was diagnosed as **wanderlust**.

## DIRECTIONS: Draw a cartoon to illustrate the word beneath each box.

| | | |
|---|---|---|
| | | |
| **transgress** | **tawdry** | **stalemate** |

# FILL-IT-OUT

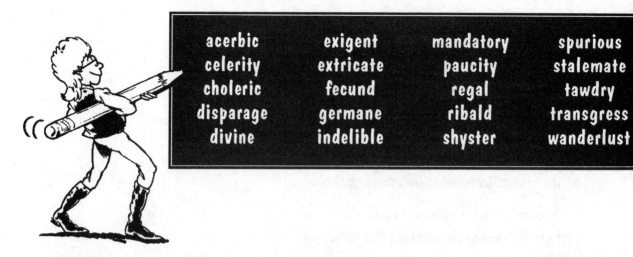

| acerbic | exigent | mandatory | spurious |
| celerity | extricate | paucity | stalemate |
| choleric | fecund | regal | tawdry |
| disparage | germane | ribald | transgress |
| divine | indelible | shyster | wanderlust |

**DIRECTIONS:** If these sentences look familiar, they are. You've just studied them in the Vocabulary section — but in a different order. Now they're scrambled, so to check your recall, fill in all the deleted SAT words.

1. "Come on, mate - it's getting late!
   Let's call it a draw and end this _____ ."

2. He was bewildered, but she was furious,
   when the jeweler informed them that the diamond was _____ .

3. With her unrefined manners and terrible taste,
   she was called " _____ Audrey" right to her face.

4. It was clear from her sexy, sultry dress,
   that Delilah intended for Samson to _____ .

5. Wanda's lust for travel was diagnosed as _____ .

6. Commanders' mandates are _____ ; so obey what they say.

7. The barber said, with a knowledgeable air,
   "Baldness, my friends, is a _____ of hair."

6

8. The king of birds is the _____ eagle.

9. On T.V., the comic was funny and clean,
   but his nightclub act was _____ and obscene.

10. The sly _____ 's shady shenanigans
    landed him in jail without any bail.

11. The lemon's _____ , bitter taste
    made Mim's mouth pucker in distaste.

12. The celebrity moved with _____ to escape
    the autograph hounds.

13. Carl's _____ boss was constantly cranky and cantankerous.

14. Gossip columnists will _____ and defame,
    to get the poop for a scoop on any hot name.

15. "A penny for your thoughts," was a saying at one time;
    but to _____ your thoughts today, would cost even more than a dime!

16. Access to the exit is _____ in an emergency.

17. It's tricky to _____ yourself from a sticky situation.

18. I'll get good crops, the farmer reckoned,
    'cause this here land is so fertile and _____ .

19. Whether it's germs, Germans, or gerbils,
    all facts must pertain and be _____ .

20. The fender bender made an _____ dent in Troy's Toyota.

# CHECK-IT-OUT

**DIRECTIONS:** Hopefully, your recall of these first 20 words is no longer evanescent. Here's your chance to CHECK-IT-OUT. Look at the definitions and underline the appropriate SAT word.

1.   transgress; to sin, to trespass
     a) extricate        b) impinge        c) intuit        d) asperse

2.   disparage; to degrade
     a) disengage        b) overstep        c) calumniate        d) disembroil

3.   choleric; grouchy
     a) bilious        b) acerbic        c) fructiferous        d) apposite

4.   spurious; counterfeit
     a) pivotal        b) flagrant        c) ersatz        d) irreverent

5.   paucity; shortage
     a) impasse        b) dearth        c) legerity        d) deadlock

6.   tawdry; gaudy
     a) brazen        b) caustic        c) sour        d) acerbic

7.   indelible; permanent
     a) simulated        b) immutable        c) prescriptive        d) irreverent

8.   regal; royal
     a) crucial        b) sovereign        c) fertile        d) tart

9.   ribald; vulgar
     a) perspective        b) scurrilous        c) pivotal        d) querulous

10.  divine; to predict
     a) intuit        b) extricate        c) overstep        d) disengage

# ODD-MAN-OUT

**DIRECTIONS:** Odds are, you'll find this a real challenge.
Three words belong and one does not.  Your job is to choose
the **ODD-MAN-OUT.**  Underline the word in each row that does not belong.

1.   a) germane        b) apposite       c) relevant        d) pungent

2.   a) tawdry         b) garish         c) caustic         d) brazen

3.   a) divine         b) impinge        c) intuit          d) augur

4.   a) asperse        b) malign         c) extricate       d) calumniate

5.   a) choleric       b) fruitful       c) irascible       d) bilious

6.   a) pungent        b) spurious       c) simulated       d) supposititious

7.   a) indelible      b) irreparable    c) imperial        d) immutable

8.   a) fecund         b) fertile        c) prescriptive    d) fructiferous

9.   a) tart           b) scurrilous     c) acerbate        d) caustic

10.  a) immutable      b) crucial        c) importunate     d) exigent

11.  a) celerity       c) legerity       c) velocity        d) obligatory

12.  a) paucity        c) sparsity       c) stalemate       d) dearth

9

# CLASSIFIEDS

**DIRECTIONS:** Let your fingers do the walking and your pencil do the talking. Use the alphabetized vocabulary to help you complete the VERBAL and VISUAL exercises.

| | | |
|---|---|---|
| 1. acerbate | 13. extricate | 25. regal |
| 2. acerbic | 14. fecund | 26. ribald |
| 3. asperse | 15. germane | 27. scurrilous |
| 4. bilious | 16. indelible | 28. shyster |
| 5. celerity | 17. irascible | 29. spurious |
| 6. calumniate | 18. legerity | 30. stalemate |
| 7. choleric | 19. mandatory | 31. tawdry |
| 8. coarse | 20. malign | 32. tart |
| 9. disparage | 21. obscene | 33. transgress |
| 10. dispatch | 22. paucity | 34. velocity |
| 11. divine | 23. pungent | 35. wanderlust |
| 12. exigent | 24. querulous | |

## VERBAL CATEGORIES

Pick the appropriate words for each group from the vocabulary list above.

**SPEEDY WORDS**

_____

_____

_____

_____

**CRANKY WORDS**

_____

_____

_____

_____

**X-RATED WORDS**

_____

_____

_____

_____

## VISUAL CATEGORIES

**DIRECTIONS:** Find the sentence that fits each cartoon.
Write the target word in box, and list all it's synonyms beneath the cartoon.

_____

_____

_____

Guess Who's On The Outs?
Bert & Ernie!

Ms. Pinky Tells All-
"My Lashes Are Fake!"

Big Bird Jailed
In Cookie Raid!

_____

_____

_____

# DRAW YOUR OWN CARTOON

**DIRECTIONS:** Pick your own word, and draw your own cartoon!

| celerity |
| :---: |

# AND NOW A NEW MYSTERY WORD TO START YOU OFF

# LESSON 2

Fill in the mystery word when you come to the sentence about Fredda.

The scared cat felt better when Fredda _____ her setter.

# VOCABULARY

1. **adapt** (uh daapt') v.

   *to adjust, acclimatize, accommodate, resign, reconcile*

   The stray kitten was adept at **adapting**
   to his new, adoptive, mongrel Mom.

2. **colloquial** (koh loh' kwee uhl) adj.

   *eveyday talk, vernacular, jargon, lingo*

   When the Queen uses the King's English, she asks, "How do you do?"
   She'd never use the **colloquial**, "Hi, how goes it with you?"

3. **din** (din) n.

   *continuous noise, clamor, racket*

   The noisy **din** in the diner disturbed the hungry diners.

4. **evanescent** (eh' vah ness' ent) adj.

   *fleeting, vanishing, transient, transitory, ephemeral*

   The rainbow was so lovely, I wished it would stay;
   but alas, it was **evanescent** and soon faded away.

5. **extemporaneous** (ex tem' por ay' nee us) adj.

   *unrehearsed, improvised, impromptu*

   If your speech is **extemporaneous**,
   think fast — be spontaneous.

## DIRECTIONS: Draw a cartoon to illustrate the word beneath each box.

| | | |
|---|---|---|
| adapt | din | evanescent |

13

6. **fetter** (feh' ter) v.

>*to restrain, secure, shackle, manacle, tether*

The scared cat felt better when Fredda **fettered** her setter.

7. **flaccid** (flaa' sid) adj.

>*flabby, limp, slack, lax*

Felix's **flaccid** handshake makes me think of a limp, wet noodle.

8. **horde** (hord) n.

>*a crowd, swarm, panoply, legion, galaxy, spate, deluge*

A **horde** of hungry locusts sated themselves
on the succulent seedlings.

9. **imbibe** (im bibe') v.

>*to drink, guaff, guzzle*

If you **imbibe**, don't dribe!

10. **incorrigible** (in car' rih jih bul) adj.

>*hopeless, confirmed, intractable, refractory, irreparable*

Cantankerous Carl was a chronically, **incorrigible**, cranky kid.

## DIRECTIONS: Draw a cartoon to illustrate the word beneath each box.

| | | |
|---|---|---|
| | | |

**flaccid**  **horde**  **imbibe**

11. **inter** (in ter') v.

   *to bury, entomb, inhume, sepulture*

   If one is **interred**, it can surely be inferred ... the poor sucker's dead.

12. **lascivious** (laa sih' vee us) adj.

   *lustful, lewd, obscene, lecherous*

   Lucy's lustful, **lascivious** ways
   make her lovers dazed for days.

13. **libertine** (lih' ber teen) n.

   *womanizer, philanderer, seducer, lecher*

   Larry was a **libertine** who tried to take
   many liberties to seduce lovely "ladies."

14. **lithe** (lythe) adj.

   *graceful, bending easily, agile, supple, willowy*

   The **lithe** lioness leaped through the forest as gracefully as a ballerina.

15. **melée** (may' lay) n.

   *confused fight, commotion, tumult, fracas, brawl*

   May was mauled and manhandled in the wild **melée** of the mob.

## DIRECTIONS: Draw a cartoon to illustrate the word beneath each box.

|  |  |  |
|---|---|---|
| inter | lithe | melée |

15

16. **noxious** (nok' shus) adj.

    *unhealthy, unsavory, virulent, pestiferous*

    The **noxious** fumes made everyone nauseous.

17. **paltry** (pawl'tree) adj.

    *meager, exiguous, scrawny, puny*

    Return that pitifully **paltry** poultry ...
    it looks like a sick chick!!

18. **sanction** (sank' shun) n.

    *law, decree;* v. *to consent, ratify, countenance, esteem*

    A.A.'s **sanctions sanction** sobriety.

19. **vilify** (vih' ilh fie) v.

    *to slander, denigrate, revile, berate, vituperate*

    Politics becomes a vile game
    when opponents **vilify** each other's name.

20. **waive** (wave) v.

    *to give up, forgo, yield, cede, forswear*

    The surfer **waived** his wave with a wave.


## DIRECTIONS: Draw a cartoon to illustrate the word beneath each box.

| | | |
|---|---|---|
| **noxious** | **paltry** | **waive** |

# FILL-IT-OUT

```
adapt            fetter          inter           noxious
colloquial       flaccid         lascivious      paltry
din              horde           libertine       sanction
evanescent       imbibe          lithe           vilify
extemporaneous   incorrigible    melée           waive
```

**DIRECTIONS:** If these sentences look familiar, they are. You've just studied them in the Vocabulary section — but in a different order. Now they're scrambled, so to check your recall, fill in all the deleted SAT words.

1. If one is _____ , it can surely be inferred...the poor sucker's dead.

2. Lucy's lustful, _____ ways
make her lovers dazed for days.

3. Larry was a _____ who took many liberties
to seduce lovely "ladies."

4. The _____ lioness leaped through the forest
as gracefully as a ballerina.

5. May was mauled and manhandled in the wild _____ of the mob.

6. The _____ fumes made everyone nauseous.

7. Return that pitifully _____ poultry...
it looks like a sick chick.

8.  A.A.'s _____ _____ sobriety.

9.  Politics becomes a vile game
    when opponents _____ each other's name.

10. The surfer _____ his wave with a wave.

11. The stray kitten was adept at _____
    to his new, adoptive, mongrel Mom.

12. When the Queen uses the King's English, she asks, "How do you do?"
    She'd never use the _____ , "Hi, how goes it with you?"

13. The noisy _____ in the diner disturbed the hungry diners.

14. The rainbow was so lovely, I wished it would stay;
    but alas, it was _____ and soon faded away.

15. If your speech is _____ , think fast — be spontaneous.

16. The scared cat felt better when Fredda _____ her setter.

17. Felix's _____ handshake makes me think
    of a limp, wet noodle.

18. A _____ of hungry locusts sated themselves
    on the succulent seedlings.

19. If you _____ , don't dribe.

20. Cantankerous Carl was a chronically, _____ , cranky kid.

18

# CHECK-IT-OUT

DIRECTIONS:  Hopefully, your recall of these first 20 words is no longer evanescent. Here's your chance to CHECK-IT-OUT.  Look at the definitions and underline the appropriate SAT word.

1. horde; a crowd
   a) quaff
   b) spate
   c) jargon
   d) clamor

2. vernacular; everyday talk
   a) colloquial
   b) impromptu
   c) philanderer
   d) libertine

3. improvised; unrehearsed
   a) supple
   b) refractory
   c) lax
   d) extemporaneous

4. waive; to give up
   a) yield
   b) revile
   c) inhume
   d) secure

5. flabby; flaccid
   a) lewd
   b) lax
   c) willowy
   d) exiguous

6. adapt; adjust
   a) secure
   b) acclimatize
   c) guzzle
   d) revile

7. clamor; continuous noise
   a) din
   b) panoply
   c) lecher
   d) brawl

8. secure; restrain
   a) quaff
   b) fetter
   c) sepulture
   d) cede

9. sanction; consent
   a) ratify
   b) berate
   c) forswear
   d) shackle

10. noxious; unhealthy
    a) lax
    b) puny
    c) virulent
    d) transient

# ODD-MAN-OUT

**DIRECTIONS:** Odds are, you'll find this a real challenge.
Three words belong and one does not. Your job is to choose
the ODD-MAN-OUT. Underline the word in each row that does not belong.

1.  a) horde        b) fracas        c) panoply        d) deluge

2.  a) lewd         b) lascivious    c) supple         d) lecherous

3.  a) flaccid      b) puny          c) limp           d) lax

4.  a) imbibe       b) quaff         c) guzzle         d) inhume

5.  a) vilify       b) revile        c) esteem         d) vituperate

6.  a) transient    b) evanescent    c) ephemeral      d) impromptu

7.  a) lithe        b) agile         c) willowy        d) noxious

8.  a) fetter       b) manacle       c) resign         d) tether

9.  a) paltry       b) scrawny       c) puny           d) transitory

10. a) adapt        b) inter         c) acclimatize    d) reconcile

11. a) din          b) clamor        c) spate          d) racket

12. a) libertine    b) seducer       c) lecher         d) jargon

# CLASSIFIEDS

**DIRECTIONS:** Let your fingers do the walking and your pencil do the talking. Use the alphabetized vocabulary to help you complete the VERBAL and VISUAL exercises.

1. adapt
2. agile
3. berate
4. colloquial
5. din
6. denigrate
7. intomb
8. evanescent
9. extemporaneous
10. exiguous
11. fetter
12. flaccid
13. imbibe
14. incorrigible
15. inhume
16. inter
17. horde
18. lascivious
19. libertine
20. lithe
21. manacle
22. melée
23. noxious
24. paltry
25. puny
26. revile
27. sanction
28. scrawny
29. secure
30. sepulture
31. supple
32. tether
33. vilify
34. waive
35. willowy

## VERBAL CATEGORIES

Pick the appropriate words for each group from the vocabulary list above.

| 6 FEET UNDER WORDS | BAD MOUTH WORDS | ALL TIED UP WORDS |
|---|---|---|
| _____ | _____ | _____ |
| _____ | _____ | _____ |
| _____ | _____ | _____ |
| _____ | _____ | _____ |

## VISUAL CATEGORIES

**DIRECTIONS:** Find the sentence which fits each cartoon.
Write the target word in the box, and list all it's synonyms beneath the cartoon.

# DRAW YOUR OWN CARTOON

## DIRECTIONS: Pick your own word, and draw your own cartoon!

| inter | |
|---|---|

# AND NOW A NEW MYSTERY WORD TO START YOU OFF

# LESSON 3

Fill in the mystery word when you come to the sentence about the misers.

_____ misers avidly hoard their money.

# VOCABULARY

1. **altercation** (all' ter kay' shun) n.

   *quarrel, wrangle, contention, litigation*

   Angry **altercations** can alter the best of vacations.

2. **artifact** (arr' tih fact) n.

   *thing, dohickey; product, handiwork, relic*

   "Art, is it a fact that this **artifact** is, in fact, a work of art?"

3. **avaricious** (aa' vuh rih' shus) adj.

   *greedy, covetous, mercenary, rapacious*

   **Avaricious** misers avidly hoard their money.

4. **cognizant** (kahg' nih zent) adj.

   *aware, knowing, privy, percipient, sentient*

   Poor Humpty wasn't **cognizant** he'd had a fall.
   When he saw his shattered shell, he had no recall.

5. **congenital** (kun jen' ih tuhl) adj.

   *by birth, genetically, innate, inbred, instinctive*

   Genes are **congenital** — they're born, not worn.

## DIRECTIONS: Draw a cartoon to illustrate the word beneath each box.

| | | |
|---|---|---|
| **artifact** | **avaricious** | **congenital** |

6. **copious** (koh' pee us) adj.

*overabundant, **ample, voluminous, diffuse***

When coping with **copious** flab and fat,

your salvation's starvation — and the exercise mat.

7. **expedient** (ex pee' dee ent) adj.

*helpful, **advantageous, auspicious, efficacious***

It's **expedient** to study before an exam;

then you won't panic and need to cram.

8. **furtive** (fer' tiv) adj.

*sneaky, **stealthy, covert***

When Cheatin' Chuck had a chance, he gave his test notes a **furtive** glance.

9. **imperial** (im peer' ee uhl) adj.

*majestic, **monarchal, regal, sovereign***

When Zeus gave his **imperial** head a shake,

Earth was rocked by a gigantic quake.

10. **lode** (lode) n.

*rich source, **gold mine, staple, fount, quarry***

King Midas had a golden touch,

but using his kid as a **lode** was a bit too much.

## DIRECTIONS: Draw a cartoon to illustrate the word beneath each box.

| | | |
|---|---|---|
| | | |

**copious**       **furtive**       **imperial**

11. **prone** (prohn) adj.

   *tends to, tendency, horizontal ;* n. *propensity*

   Nero was **prone** to eat grapes while propped up in a semi-**prone** position.

12. **putrid** (pyou' trid) adj.

   *foul smelling, malodorous; revolting, odious*

   The **putrid** smell from the sewer made Luke puke.

13. **quixotic** (kwik sah' tik) adj.

   *romantic, transcendental, visionary*

   To fall in love is **quixotic**, romantic, and very erotic.

14. **rectify** (rek' tih fy) v.

   *to correct, remedy, redress, amend, emend*

   When the biologist changed himself into a fly,
   it was a mistake he couldn't **rectify**.

15. **repartée** (reh' par tay) n.

   *witticism, pleasantry, levity, quip, retort*

   **Repartée** is what you say when you say what you say in a quick, clever way.

## DIRECTIONS: Draw a cartoon to illustrate the word beneath each box.

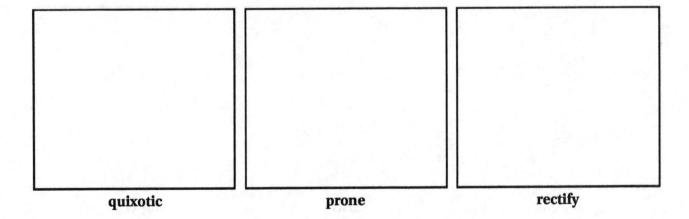

| quixotic | prone | rectify |

16. **reverberate** (ree ver' ber ate) v.

   *to echo, resound, rebound, resonate*

   The Swiss yokel's yodel **reverberated** through the Alps.

17. **servile** (ser' vile) adj.

   *slavish, obsequious, deferential, fawning*

   Cinderella's stepmother kept Cindy **servile** and submissive.

18. **vacuous** (vak' you us) adj.

   *empty, vapid, trivial, vacant, banal*

   The **vacuous** chatter of the verbose ventriloquist
   made him seem as dumb as his dummy.

19. **vitriolic** (vih' tree ah' lik) adj.

   *savagely hostile, rancorous, acerbic, acrimonious, caustic*

   The vicious vampire voiced his **vitriolic**
   curse, snarling, "I vant to suck your blood."

20. **wince** (wince) v.

   *to retreat from pain or danger, flinch, cringe, recoil*

   A fierce, fiery dragon can make even a proud prince **wince**.

**DIRECTIONS: Draw a cartoon to illustrate the word beneath each box.**

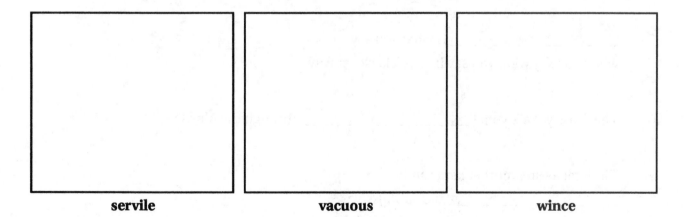

| servile | vacuous | wince |

# FILL-IT-OUT

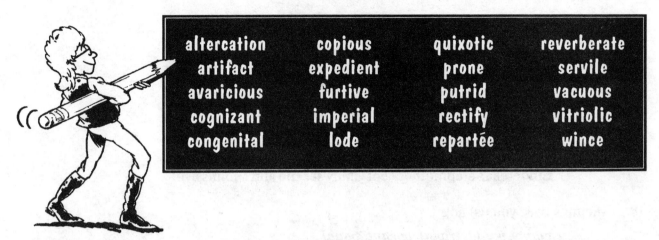

| | | | |
|---|---|---|---|
| altercation | copious | quixotic | reverberate |
| artifact | expedient | prone | servile |
| avaricious | furtive | putrid | vacuous |
| cognizant | imperial | rectify | vitriolic |
| congenital | lode | repartée | wince |

DIRECTIONS: If these sentences look familiar, they are. You've just studied them in the Vocabulary section — but in a different order. Now they're scrambled, so to check your recall, fill in all the deleted SAT words.

1.  To fall in love is _____ , romantic, and very erotic.

2.  Nero was _____ to eat grapes while propped up
    in a semi- _____ position.

3.  The _____ smell from the sewer made Luke puke.

4.  When the biologist changed himself into a fly,
    it was a mistake he couldn't _____ .

5.  _____ is what you say
    when you say what you say in a quick, clever way.

6.  The Swiss yokel's yodel _____ through the Alps.

7.  Cinderella's stepmother kept Cindy
    _____ and submissive.

8. The _____ chatter of the verbose ventriloquist made him seem as dumb as his dummy.

9. The vicious vampire voiced his _____ curse, snarling, "I vant to suck your blood."

10. A fierce, fiery dragon can make even a proud prince _____

11. Angry _____ can alter the best of vacations.

12. "Art, is it a fact that this _____ is, in fact, a work of art?"

13. _____ misers avidly hoard their money.

14. Poor Humpty wasn't _____ he'd had a fall. When he saw his shattered shell, he had no recall.

15. Genes are _____ — they're born, not worn!

16. When coping with _____ flab and fat, your salvation's starvation — and the exercise mat.

17. It's _____ to study before an exam; then you won't panic and need to cram.

18. When Cheatin' Chuck had the chance, he gave his test notes a _____ glance.

19. When Zeus gave his _____ head a shake, Earth was rocked by a gigantic quake.

20. King Midas had a golden touch, but using his kid as a _____ was a bit too much.

# CHECK-IT-OUT

**DIRECTIONS:** Hopefully, your recall of these first 20 words is no longer evanescent. Here's your chance to CHECK-IT-OUT. Look at the definitions and underline the appropriate SAT word.

1. reverberate; echo
   a) resonate     b) recoil     c) redress     d) cringe

2. servile; slavish
   a) obsequious     b) rapacious     c) banal     d) acerbic

3. avaricious; greedy
   a) percipient     b) rapacious     c) instinctive     d) voluminous

4. repartée; witticism
   a) litigation     b) quip     c) relic     d) lode

5. altercation; quarrel
   a) staple     b) contention     c) quip     d) artifact

6. imperial; majestic
   a) sovereign     b) supine     c) odious     d) deferential

7. quixotic; romantic
   a) servile     b) transcendental     c) banal     d) caustic

8. wince; retreat from pain
   a) emend     b) flinch     c) remedy     d) rectify

9. vacuous; empty
   a) rancorous     b) banal     c) covetous     d) rapacious

10. congenital; by birth
    a) stealthy     b) efficacious     c) instinctive     d) vacant

# ODD-MAN-OUT

**DIRECTIONS:** Odds are, you'll find this a real challenge.
Three words belong and one does not. Your job is to choose
the ODD-MAN-OUT. Underline the word in each row that does not belong.

1.  a) congenital      b) innate         c) inbred          d) supine

2.  a) expedient       b) efficacious    c) voluminous      d) auspicious

3.  a) avaricious      b) covetous       c) innate          d) rapacious

4.  a) repartée        b) levity         c) rebound         d) quip

5.  a) dearth          b) extol          c) adulate         d) laud

6.  a) paucity         b) qualm          c) want            d) scantiness

7.  a) gull            b) doff           c) denude          d) bare

8.  a) ephemeral       b) transitory     c) anachronistic   d) illusory

9.  a) maladroit       b) specious       c) ungainly        d) bungling

10. a) divulge         b) air            c) disclose        d) depreciate

11. a) deceive         b) beguile        c) divest          d) hoax

12. a) immure          b) obliterate     c) expunge         d) efface

# CLASSIFIEDS

**DIRECTIONS:** Let your fingers do the walking and your pencil do the talking. Use the alphabetized vocabulary to help you complete the VERBAL and VISUAL exercises.

1. altercation
2. ample
3. artifact
4. avaricious
5. banal
6. cognizant
7. congenital
8. copious
9. covert
10. covetous
11. diffuse
12. expedient

13. furtive
14. imperial
15. lode
16. mercenary
17. percipient
18. privy
19. prone
20. putrid
21. quixotic
22. rapacious
23. rectify
24. repartée

25. reverberate
26. sentient
27. servile
28. sneaky
29. stealthy
30. vacant
31. vacuous
32. vapid
33. vitriolic
34. voluminous
35. wince

## VERBAL CATEGORIES

Pick the appropriate words for each group from the vocabulary list above.

**MONEY-HUNGRY WORDS**

_____

_____

_____

_____

**KNOW IT ALL WORDS**

_____

_____

_____

_____

**JAMES BOND/007 WORDS**

_____

_____

_____

_____

## VISUAL CATEGORIES

**DIRECTIONS:** Find the sentence which fits each cartoon.
Write the target word in the box, and list all it's synonyms beneath the cartoon.

_____

_____

_____

_____

_____

_____

# DRAW YOUR OWN CARTOON

**DIRECTIONS:** Pick your own word, and draw your own cartoon!

| congenital | |
|---|---|

# LESSON 4

Fill in the mystery word when you come to the sentence about the skunk.

You can't _____ the fact that the skunk stunk.

# VOCABULARY

1.  **allay** (uh lay') v.

    *to soothe, **placate, pacify, assuage***

    **Allay** your anxieties, and put your fears to rest.
    With PowerWords, you'll best any test.

2.  **conjure** (kahn' jer) v.

    *to call up spirits, **trick, beguile, dupe, invoke***

    To **conjure** up the spirit of big, obese Wanda,
    the medium offered pasta, coaxing, "Manja, manja."

3.  **crass** (krass) adj.

    *unrefined, **gross, coarse, uncouth***

    If you're vulgar and **crass**, you've got no class.

4.  **debunk** (dih bunk') v.

    *to expose as untrue, **disillusion, disabuse, disillude***

    You can't **debunk** the fact that the skunk stunk.

5.  **feasible** (feez' uh buhl) adj.

    *possible, **plausible, credible, conceivable***

    Weary and teary, Paula pleaded, "Be reasonable.
    To finish by five is simply not **feasible**."

## DIRECTIONS: Draw a cartoon to illustrate the word beneath each box.

|  |  |  |
| --- | --- | --- |
| **conjure** | **crass** | **debunk** |

6. **halcyon** (hal' see on) adj.

     *calm, pacific, tranquil, serene, concordant*

     The sea was so tranquil and calm,

     it could only be described as **halcyon**.

7. **heinous** (hay' nus) adj.

     *hateful, base, vile, nefarious, iniquitous*

     Don't be **heinous**, your highness —we'll starve if you fine us.

8. **impromptu** (im promp' too) adj.

     *unplanned, improvised, extemporaneous, spontaneous*

     When the teacher sprang the **impromptu** quiz,

     no one passed, except Liz, the class whizz.

9. **inception** (in sehp' shun) n.

     *a beginning, genesis, inchoation, incipience*

     Conception is the **inception** of life.

10. **mandate** (man' date) n.

     *a command, interdict, injunction, referendum*

     In '88, the voters' **mandate** was clear,

     and Bush became President later that year.

## DIRECTIONS: Draw a cartoon to illustrate the word beneath each box.

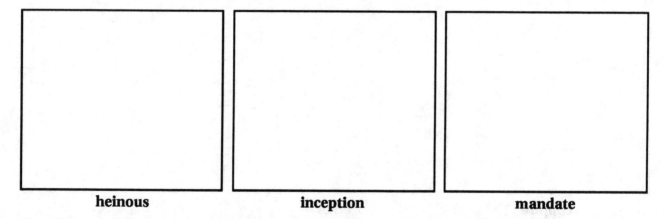

    **heinous**           **inception**           **mandate**

11. **meander** (mee an' der) v.

   *to stroll, ramble, saunter, peregrinate*

   Willy **meandered** mindlessly along the winding Mississippi.

12. **pernicious** (per nish' us) adj.

   *deadly, noxious, toxic, lethal*

   Captain Hook's **pernicious** plan
   was to kidnap Wendy and kill Peter Pan.

13. **punctilious** (punk till' ee us) adj.

   *punctual, expeditious, meticulous*

   Priscilla preferred **punctilious** nerds as dates,
   over gorgeous hunks, who were usually late.

14. **quack** (qwak) n.

   *phony, fraud, imposter, charlatan*

   Mr. Bird impersonated so many doctors that his
   misdiagnosed patients called him Dr. **Quack**.

15. **quaint** (kwaint) adj.

   *unusual, not stylish, old fashioned, singular*

   **Quaint** dresses are outdated — much too long;
   short minis are in and going strong.

## DIRECTIONS: Draw a cartoon to illustrate the word beneath each box.

| | | |
|---|---|---|
| | | |
| **meander** | **pernicious** | **quaint** |

16. **querulous** (kweh' ruh lus) adj.

 *irritable, peevish, plangent, petulant, plaintive*

 Cranky, **querulous** Quentin was quick to quarrel with everyone.

17. **sparse** (sparce) adj.

 *scarce, scant, exiguous, meager*

 Oxygen is **sparse** on Mars.

18. **tryst** (trist) n.

 *an appointed meeting for lovers, rendezvous, assignation*

 Juliet told Romeo the time for their **tryst**
 was to be later that night, when she wouldn't be missed.

19. **verbose** (very bose') adj.

 *wordy, loquacious, voluble, garrulous, prolix*

 Talkative Tilly was terribly **verbose**.

20. **worst** (werst) v.

 *to defeat, to best, beat, trounce, lick*

 To **worst** your opponent, you must play your best.

## DIRECTIONS: Draw a cartoon to illustrate the word beneath each box.

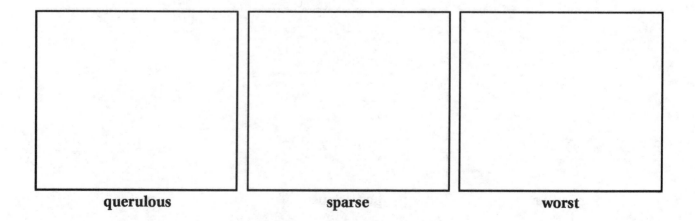

| querulous | sparse | worst |

38

# FILL-IT-OUT

| | | | |
|---|---|---|---|
| allay | halcyon | meander | querulous |
| conjure | heinous | pernicious | sparse |
| crass | impromptu | punctilious | tryst |
| debunk | inception | quack | verbose |
| feasible | mandate | quaint | worst |

**DIRECTIONS:** If these sentences look familiar, they are. You've just studied them in the Vocabulary lesson—but in a different order. Now they're scrambled, so to check your recall, fill in all the deleted SAT words.

1. Willy _____ mindlessly along the winding Mississippi.

2. Captain Hook's _____ plan
   was to kidnap Wendy and kill Peter Pan.

3. Priscilla preferred _____ nerds as dates,
   over gorgeous hunks, who were usually late.

4. Mr. Bird impersonated so many doctors that his
   misdiagnosed patients called him Dr. _____ .

5. _____ dresses are outdated—much too long.
   Short minis are in and going strong.

6. Cranky, _____ Quentin was quick to quarrel with everyone.

7. Oxygen is _____ on Mars.

39

8. Juliet told Romeo the time for their _____
   was to be later that night, when she wouldn't be missed.

9. Talkative Tilly was terribly _____ .

10. To _____ your opponent, you must play your best.

11. _____ your anxieties, and put your fears to rest.
    With PowerWords, you'll best any test.

12. To _____ up the spirit of big, obese Wanda,
    the medium offered pasta, coaxing "Manja, manja."

13. If you're vulgar and _____ , you've got no class.

14. You can't _____ the fact that the skunk stunk.

15. Weary and teary, Paula pleaded, "Be reasonable.
    To finish by five is simply not _____ ."

16. The sea was so tranquil and calm,
    it could only be described as _____ .

17. Don't be _____ , your highness.
    We'll starve if you fine us!

18. When the teacher sprang the _____ quiz,
    no one passed, except Liz, the class whizz.

19. Conception is the _____ of life.

20. In '88, the voters' _____ was clear,
    and Bush became President later that year.

# CHECK-IT-OUT

DIRECTIONS:  Hopefully, your recall of these first 20 words is no longer evanescent.
Here's your chance to CHECK-IT-OUT.  Look at the definitions
and underline the appropriate SAT word.

1.    querulous; irritable
      a) prolix              b) petulant          c) exiguous          d) meticulous

2.    crass; unrefined
      a) credible            b) coarse            c) serene            d) vile

3.    inception; a beginning
      a) injunction          b) pacify            c) interdict         d) inchoation

4.    heinous; hateful
      a) toxic               b) quaint            c) nefarious         d) peevish

5.    halcyon; calm
      a) pacific             b) meticulous        c) plaintive         d) scant

6.    allay; to soothe
      a) dupe                b) placate           c) debunk            d) trounce

7.    feasible; possible
      a) punctilious         b) base              c) lethal            d) conceivable

8.    pernicious; deadly
      a) expeditious         b) noxious           c) singular          d) peevish

9.    conjure; to call up spirits
      a) saunter             b) assuage           c) invoke            d) disillude

10.   tryst; a meeting for lovers
      a) referendum          b) assignation       c) genesis           d) charlatan

# ODD-MAN-OUT

**DIRECTIONS:** Odds are, you'll find this a real challenge.
Three words belong and one does not. Your job is to choose
the ODD-MAN-OUT. Underline the word in each row that does not belong.

1. a) punctilious     b) expeditious     c) meticulous     d) spontaneous

2. a) meander     b) beguile     c) ramble     d) peregrinate

3. a) sparse     b) gross     c) exiguous     d) scant

4. a) heinous     b) nefarious     c) voluble     d) iniquitous

5. a) genesis     b) inchoation     c) inception     d) mandate

6. a) feasible     b) serene     c) plausible     d) credible

7. a) fraud     b) charlatan     c) injunction     d) quack

8. a) saunter     b) debunk     c) disabuse     d) disillude

9. a) pernicious     b) noxious     c) prolix     d) toxic

10. a) crass     b) concordant     c) uncouth     d) coarse

11. a) worst     b) beat     c) ramble     d) best

12 a) plausible     b) querulous     c) plangent     d) plaintive

# CLASSIFIEDS

DIRECTIONS: Let your fingers do the walking and your pencil do the talking. Use the alphabetized vocabulary to help you complete the VERBAL and VISUAL exercises

1. allay
2. assuage
3. base
4. conjure
5. crass
6. debunk
7. feasible
8. garrulous
9. genesis
10. halcyon
11. heinous
12. impromptu

13. inception
14. inchoation
15. incipience
16. iniquitous
17. loquacious
18. mandate
19. meander
20. nefarious
21. pacify
22. peregrinate
23. pernicious
24. placate

25. punctilious
26. quack
27. quaint
28. querulous
29. ramble
30. sparse
31. saunter
32. tryst
33. verbose
34. voluble
35. worst

## VERBAL CATEGORIES

Pick the appropriate words for each group from the vocabulary list above.

**FEEL BETTER WORDS**

_____

_____

_____

_____

**TAKE A HIKE WORDS**

_____

_____

_____

_____

**BLAB BLAB BLAB WORDS**

_____

_____

_____

_____

## VISUAL CATEGORIES

DIRECTIONS: Find the sentence which fits each cartoon.
Write the target word in the box, and list all it's synonyms beneath the cartoon.

_____

_____

_____

_____

_____

_____

# DRAW YOUR OWN CARTOON

## DIRECTIONS: Pick your own word, and draw your own cartoon!

halcyon

# LESSON 5

Fill in the mystery word when you come to the sentence about Clyde.

Terrified Clyde tried to hide
when the charging lion left his _____.

# VOCABULARY

1.  **affront** (uh frunt') v.

    *to oppose, **confront, front;*** n. ***insult, offense, injury***

    The huge Sumo wrestler gave a great grunt,

    when he faced the opponent he had to **affront**.

2.  **blasé** (blah zay') adj.

    *bored, **jaded, oversated, languid, apathetic***

    The bored, **blasé** boy had everything — plus a bad case of the "blahs."

3.  **coerce** (ko erse') v.

    *to force, to bully, **compel, impel, intimidate***

    The mugger **coerced** the nurse to give up her purse.

4.  **contrition** (kun trih' shun) n.

    *regret, **remorse, compunction, attrition***

    Evildoers, who show no **contrition**,

    are often doomed to hell and perdition.

5.  **deleterious** (deh' leh teer' ee us) adj.

    *harmful, **detrimental, baneful, scatheful***

    It's not so mysterious; crack is definitely **deleterious**.

## DIRECTIONS: Draw a cartoon to illustrate the word beneath each box.

|  |  |  |
| --- | --- | --- |
|  |  |  |
| **affront** | **blasé** | **contrition** |

46

6. **despot** (des' paht) n.

  *tyrant, martinet, autocrat, arrogator*

  Dis is de spot where de good guy got shot
  by dat dastardly, decadent, evil **despot** .

7. **enigmatic** (eh' nig maa' tik) adj.

  *puzzling, inexplicable, cryptic*

  The magician's **enigmatic** tricks mystified his audience.

8. **fiat** (fee' aht) n.

  *an order, decree, mandate, edict, dictum*

  A **fiat** is not a car ... it's a decree.

9. **forgery** (for' jer ee) n.

  *fake, fabrication, counterfeit, bogus*

  "No way, George; you can't fool me.
  Leonardo never did this ... it's a **forgery**!"

10. **garrulous** (gaa' roo lus) adj.

  *talkative, verbose, loquacious, prolix, voluble*

  As **garrulous** Greta gabbed on and on,
  everyone soon was gone, gone, gone.

## DIRECTIONS: Draw a cartoon to illustrate the word beneath each box.

| | | |
|---|---|---|
| **enigmatic** | **forgery** | **garrulous** |

11. **hone** (hohn) v.

   *to sharpen, **whet, edge***

   The caveman **honed** his blade of stone,

   and deftly cut the meat off the bone.

12. **hyperbole** (hi per' boh lee) n.

   *exaggeration, **overstatement, superlative, amplification***

   Don't exaggerate, please;

   just give me the facts, no **hyperboles.**

13. **inebriate** (in ee' bree ate) v.

   *to make drunk, **intoxicate, besot***

   The **inebriated** driver couldn't walk the straight line,

   but he sobered up fast when hit with a fine.

14. **odoriferous** (oh' dor if' er us) adj.

   *smelly, **tangy, pungent, redolent***

   The **odoriferous**, spicy smells from the vendor's cart

   drew hordes of hungry New Yorkers.

15. **presage** (preh' suhj) n.

   *prediction, **presentiment, premonition, augury***

   "Beware the Ides of March!" was the soothsayer's **presage**,

   but it didn't help Caesar, 'cause he ignored the message.

## DIRECTIONS: Draw a cartoon to illustrate the word beneath each box.

| | | |
|---|---|---|
| | | |

**hone**  **inebriate**  **presage**

16. **pride** (pride) n.

>*a group of lions*

>Terrified Clyde tried to hide
>when the charging lion left his **pride**.

17. **salacious** (suh lay' shus) adj.

>*lustful, lascivious, lewd, lecherous, carnal*

>**Salacious** Sal seduced many a gal.

18. **succumb** (suh cum') v.

>*to submit, yield, acquiesce, relent, capitulate*

>When on a diet, one mustn't **succumb**
>to cakes or cookies — not even a crumb.

19. **terse** (turse) adj.

>*brief, concise, pithy, curt, succinct*

>When a verse is **terse**, it's quickly rehearsed.

20. **wisp** (wisp) n.

>*a little thing, diminutive, bantam, slip, snippet*

>Tinkerbell was such a little **wisp** of a thing,
>she loved to perch on Peter's ring.

## DIRECTIONS: Draw a cartoon to illustrate the word beneath each box.

| | | |
|---|---|---|
| **pride** | **succumb** | **wisp** |

# FILL-IT-OUT

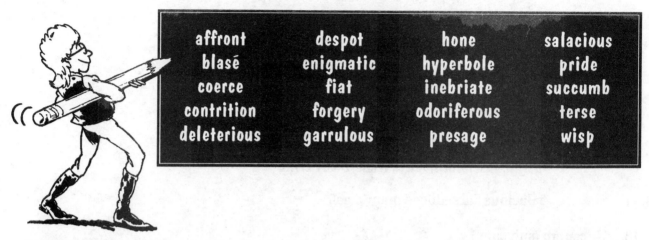

affront despot hone salacious
blasé enigmatic hyperbole pride
coerce fiat inebriate succumb
contrition forgery odoriferous terse
deleterious garrulous presage wisp

**DIRECTIONS:** If these sentences look familiar, they are. You've just studied them in the Vocabulary lesson—but in a different order. Now they're scrambled, so to check your recall, fill in all the deleted SAT words.

1. The caveman _____ his blade of stone,
and deftly cut the meat from the bone.

2. Don't exaggerate, please;
just give me the facts, no _____ .

3. The _____ driver couldn't walk the straight line,
but he sobered up fast when hit with a fine.

4. The _____ , spicy smells from the vendor's cart
drew hordes of hungry New Yorkers.

5. "Beware the Ides of March!" was the soothsayers _____ ,
but it didn't help Caesar, 'cause he ignored the message.

6. _____ Sal seduced many a gal.

7. Terrified Clyde tried to hide
when the charging lion left his _____ .

8. When on a diet, one mustn't _____
   to cakes or cookies - not even a crumb.

9. When a verse is _____ , it's quickly rehearsed.

10. Tinkerbell was such a little _____ of a thing,
    she loved to perch on Peter's ring.

11. The huge Sumo wrestler gave a great grunt
    when he faced the opponent he had to _____ .

12. The bored, _____ boy had everything — plus a bad case of the "blahs."

13. The mugger _____ the nurse to give up her purse.

14. Evildoers, who show no _____ ,
    are often doomed to hell and perdition.

15. It's not so mysterious; crack is definitely _____ .

16. Dis is de spot where de good guy got shot
    by dat dastardly, decadent, evil _____

17. The magician's _____ tricks mystified his audience.

18. A _____ is not a car ... it's a decree.

19. "No way, George; you can't fool me.
    Leonardo never did this ... it's a _____ .

20. As _____ Greta gabbed on and on,
    everyone soon was gone, gone, gone.

# CHECK-IT-OUT

**DIRECTIONS:** Hopefully, your recall of these first 20 words is no longer evanescent. Here's your chance to CHECK-IT-OUT. Look at the definitions and underline the appropriate SAT word.

1.  affront; oppose
    a) whet          b) confront      c) besot         d) relent

2.  wisp; a little thing
    a) pride         b) snippet       c) augury        d) hyperbole

3.  terse; brief
    a) concise       b) apathetic     c) lewd          d) pungent

4.  deleterious; harmful
    a) tangy         b) loquacious    c) cryptic       d) scatheful

5.  blasé; bore
    a) cryptic       b) jaded         c) baneful       d) redolent

6.  contrition; regret
    a) dictum        b) compunction   c) fabrication   d) amplification

7.  salacious; lustful
    a) languid       b) curt          c) pithy         d) lecherous

8.  coerce; to force
    a) edge          b) impel         c) hone          d) capitulate

9.  presage; prediction
    a) affront       b) offense       c) attrition     d) augury

10. despot; tyrant
    a) arrogator     b) fiat          c) decree        d) bogus

52

# ODD-MAN-OUT

**DIRECTIONS:** Odds are, you'll find this a real challenge.
Three words belong and one does not. Your job is to choose
the **ODD-MAN-OUT**. Underline the word in each row that does not belong.

1.  a) contrition        b) pride           c) compunction      d) attrition

2.  a) presage          b) wisp            c) augury           d) presentiment

3.  a) intimidate       b) succumb         c) relent           d) capitulate

4.  a) terse            b) redolent        c) succinct         d) pithy

5.  a) deleterious      b) baneful         c) detrimental      d) prolix

6.  a) odoriferous      b) tangy           c) baneful          d) redolent

7.  a) carnal           b) salacious       c) lecherous        d) deleterious

8.  a) fiat             b) contrition      c) mandate          d) edict

9.  a) enigmatic        b) inexplicable    c) lewd             d) cryptic

10. a) forgery          b) offense         c) counterfeit      d) bogus

11. a) coerce           b) inebriate       c) intoxicate       d) besot

12. a) verbose          b) capitulate      c) loquacious       d) voluble

# CLASSIFIEDS

DIRECTIONS: Let your fingers do the walking and your pencil do the talking. Use the alphabetized vocabulary to help you complete the VERBAL and VISUAL exercises.

1. belittle
1. acquiesce
2. affront
3. baneful
4. bantam
5. blasé
6. carnal
7. capitulate
8. coerce
9. contrition
10. curt
11. deleterious
12. detrimental
13. fulsome
13. despot
14. diminutive
15. enigmatic
16. fiat
17. forgery
18. garrulous
19. hone
20. hyperbole
21. inebriate
22. lascivious
23. lecherous
24. odoriferous
25. purgative
25. pithy
26. presage
27. pride
28. relent
29. salacious
31. slip
32. succumb
33. succinct
34. terse
35. wisp

## VERBAL CATEGORIES

Pick the appropriate words for each group from the vocabulary list above.

**WEE LITLE THING WORDS**

_____
_____
_____
_____

**CUT IT SHORT WORDS**

_____
_____
_____
_____

**KILLER WORDS**

_____
_____
_____
_____

## VISUAL CATEGORIES

DIRECTIONS: Find the sentence which fits each cartoon.
Write the target word in the box, and list all it's synonyms beneath the cartoon.

_____          _____
_____          _____
_____          _____

# DRAW YOUR OWN CARTOON

DIRECTIONS: Pick your own word, and draw your own cartoon!

| despot |
| --- |

# CROSSWORD PUZZLE REVIEW

# LESSON 1

ACROSS CLUES
2. to predict
7. appropriate
8. to free
9. a standstill
11. bitter, sour
14. grouchy
17. gaudy, shameless
18. desire to travel

DOWN CLUES
1. swindler
2. to degrade
3. critical
4. counterfeit
5. royal, king-like
6. to trespass; to sin
10. productive
13. required
15. permanent
16. a shortage

# LESSON 2

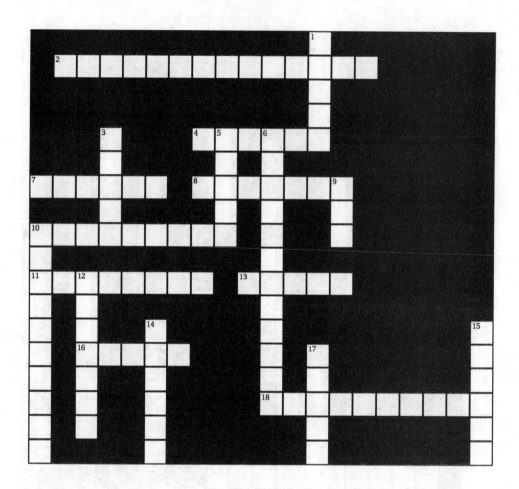

ACROSS CLUES
2. unrehearsed
4. to drink
7. slander
8. flabby
10. womanizer
11. to consent
13. graceful, bending easily
16. to bury
18. fleeting, vanishing

DOWN CLUES
1. a crowd
3. to give up
5. a confused fight
6. hopeless, beyond control
9. continuous noise
10. lustful
12. unhealthy
14. to restrain
15. meager
17. adjust

# LESSON 3

ACROSS CLUES

3. foul smelling
4. retreat from pain or danger
5. a quarrel
6. to correct
7. aware, knowing
8. greedy
13. witticism
14. rich source, gold mine
15. majestic
16. helpful

DOWN CLUES

1. horizontal
2. romantic
5. thing; product
5. to clarify
7. by birth
9. to echo
10. sneaky
11. savagely hostile
12. slavish

# LESSON 4

ACROSS CLUES
1. calm
4. call up spirits; trick
6. wordy
8. punctual
11. scarce
13. stroll
14. unusual; not stylish
15. to soothe

DOWN CLUES
2. unrefined
3. to defeat
5. an appointed
   meeting for lovers
7. phony
8. deadly
9. a beginning
10. unplanned
12. hateful
13. a command
14. irritable

# LESSON 5

ACROSS CLUES
2. puzzling
4. regret
5. a fake
6. a group of lions
8. smelly
10. to oppose; an insult
13. a little thing
15. bored
17. exaggeration
18. lustful
19. harmful

DOWN CLUES
1. to force; to bully
3. talkative
6. prediction
7. to sharpen
9. to make drunk
11. an order
12. brief
14. to submit
16. tyrant

# CLASSIFIEDS REVIEW

**DIRECTIONS:** Turn to page 63 and create your own classifieds, using the words you've learned in Lessons 1 through 5.

## SPEEDY WORDS

_____
_____
_____
_____

## CRANKY WORDS

_____
_____
_____
_____

## X-RATED WORDS

_____
_____
_____
_____

## 6 FEET UNDER WORDS

_____
_____
_____
_____

## BAD MOUTH WORDS

_____
_____
_____
_____

## ALL TIED UP WORDS

_____
_____
_____
_____

## MONEY-HUNGRY WORDS

_____
_____
_____
_____

## KNOW IT ALL WORDS

_____
_____
_____
_____

## JAMES BOND/007 WORDS

_____
_____
_____
_____

## FEEL BETTER WORDS

_____
_____
_____
_____

## TAKE A HIKE WORDS

_____
_____
_____
_____

## BLAB BLAB BLAB WORDS

_____
_____
_____
_____

## WEE LITTLE THING WORDS

_____
_____
_____
_____

## CUT IT SHORT WORDS

_____
_____
_____
_____

## KILLER WORDS

_____
_____
_____
_____

# ANSWER SHEET

## LESSON 1

**CHECK-IT-OUT**
1) b 2) c 3) a 4) c 5) b 6) a 7) b 8) b 9 b 10) a

**ODD-MAN-OUT**
1) d 2) c 3) b 4) c 5) b 6) a 7) c 8) c 9) b 10) a
11) d 12) c

**CLASSIFIEDS**
**SPEEDY** — celerity, dispatch, legerity, velocity
**CRANKY** — choleric, bilious, irascible, querulous
**X-RATED** — ribald, scurrilous, coarse, irreverent

**Picture 1** — acerbic          **Picture 2** — disparage

## LESSON 2

**CHECK-IT-OUT**
1) b 2) a 3) d 4) a 5) b 6) b 7) a 8) b 9) a 10) c

**ODD-MAN-OUT**
1) b 2) c 3) b 4) d 5) c 6) d 7) d 8) c 9) d 10) b
11) c 12) d

**CLASSIFIEDS**
**6 FEET UNDER** — inter, inhume, entomb, sepulture
**BAD MOUTH** — vilify, denigrate, berate, revile
**ALL TIED UP** — fetter, secure, manacle, tether

**Picture 1** — lithe          **Picture 2** — paltry

## LESSON 3

**CHECK-IT-OUT**
1) a 2) a 3) b 4) b 5) b 6) a 7) b 8) b 9) b 10) c

**ODD-MAN-OUT**

1) d 2) c 3) c 4) c 5) d 6) d 7) c 8) b 9) d 10) b
11) b 12) d

    **MONEY-HUNGRY** — avaricious, covetous, mercenary, rapacious
    **KNOW IT ALL** — privy, percipient, sentient
    **JAMES BOND/007** — furtive, sneaky, stealthy, covert

    **Picture 1** – copious          **Picture 2** – vacuous

# LESSON 4

**CHECK-IT-OUT**
1) b      (2) b      (3) d      (4) c      (5) a      (6) b      (7) d      (8) b      (9) c      10) b

**ODD-MAN-OUT**
1) d      2) b      3) b      4) c      5) d      6) b      7) c      8) a      9) c      10) b
11) c      12) a

**CLASSIFIEDS**
    **FEEL BETTER** — allay, assuage, pacify, placate
    **TAKE A HIKE**— meander, ramble, saunter, peregrinate
    **BLAB, BLAB, BLAB** — verbose, loquacious, voluble, garrulous

    **Picture 1** — heinous          **Picture 2** — inception

# LESSON 5

**CHECK-IT-OUT**
1) b      2) b      3) a      4) d      5) b      6) b      7) d      8) b      9) d      10) a

**ODD-MAN-OUT**
1) b      2) b      3) a      4) b      5) d      6) c      7) d      8) b      9) c      10) b
11) a      12) b

**CLASSIFIEDS**
    **WEE LITTLE THING** — wisp, diminutive, bantam, slip
    **CUT IT SHORT** — terse, succinct, curt, pithy
    **KILLER** — deleterious, detrimental, baneful, scatheful

    **Picture 1** — salacious          **Picture 2** — succumb

# CROSSWORD ANSWER SHEET

## Crossword Puzzle LESSON 1

## Crossword Puzzle LESSON 2

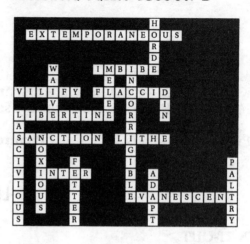

## Crossword Puzzle LESSON 3

## Crossword Puzzle LESSON 4

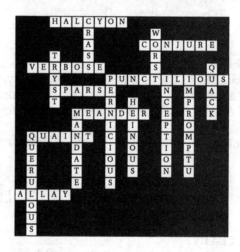

## Crossword Puzzle LESSON 5

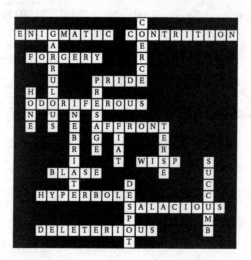

66

# POWERWORDS™ SAT® THESAURUS

**acerbic**      (adj.)      *bitter, sour*             Page   2
     acerbate
     caustic
     pungent
     tart

**adapt**      (v.)      *to adjust*             Page   13
     acclimate
     accommodate
     reconcile
     resign

**affront**      (v.)      *to oppose*             Page   46
     confront
     front
     injury      (n.)      *an insult*
     offense

**allay**      (v.)      *to soothe*             Page   35
     assuage
     pacify
     placate

**altercation**      (n.)      *quarrel*             Page   24
     contention
     litigation
     wrangle

**artifact**      (n.)      *thing, product*             Page   24
     dohickey
     handiwork
     relic

**avaricious**      (adj.)      *greedy*             Page   24
     covetous
     mercenary
     rapacious

**blasé**      (adj.)      *bored*             Page   46
     apathetic
     jaded
     languid

**celerity**      (n.)      *speed*             Page   2
     dispatch
     legerity
     velocity

| | | | | |
|---|---|---|---|---|
| **debunk**<br>  disabuse<br>  disillude<br>  disillusion | (v.) | *to expose as untrue* | Page | 35 |
| **deleterious**<br>  baneful<br>  detrimental<br>  scatheful | (adj.) | *harmful* | Page | 46 |
| **despot**<br>  arrogator<br>  autocrat<br>  martinet | (n.) | *tyrant* | Page | 47 |
| **din**<br>  clamor<br>  racket | (n.) | *continuous noise* | Page | 13 |
| **disparage**<br>  asperse<br>  calumniate<br>  discredit<br>  malign | (v.) | *to degrade* | Page | 2 |
| **divine**<br>  augur<br>  intuit | (v.) | *to predict* | Page | 2 |
| **enigmatic**<br>  cryptic<br>  inexplicable | (adj.) | *puzzling* | Page | 47 |
| **evanescent**<br>  ephemeral<br>  transient<br>  transitory | (adj.) | *fleeting, vanishing* | Page | 13 |
| **exigent**<br>  crucial<br>  importunate<br>  pivotal | (adj.) | *critical* | Page | 3 |
| **expedient**<br>  advantageous<br>  auspicious<br>  efficacious | (adj.) | *helpful* | Page | 25 |

| | | | | |
|---|---|---|---|---|
| **extemporaneous**<br>impromptu<br>improvised | (adj.) | *unrehearsed* | Page | 13 |
| **extricate**<br>disembroil<br>disengage<br>disentwine | (v.) | *to free* | Page | 3 |
| **feasible**<br>conceivable<br>credible<br>plausible | (adj.) | *possible* | Page | 35 |
| **fecund**<br>fertile<br>fructiferous<br>fruitful | (adj.) | *productive* | Page | 3 |
| **fetter**<br>manacle<br>secure<br>shackle<br>tether | (v.) | *to restrain* | Page | 14 |
| **fiat**<br>decree<br>dictum<br>edict<br>mandate | (n.) | *an order* | Page | 47 |
| **flaccid**<br>lax<br>limp<br>slack | (adj.) | *flabby* | Page | 14 |
| **forgery**<br>bogus<br>counterfeit<br>fabrication | (n.) | *fake* | Page | 47 |
| **furtive**<br>covert<br>stealthy | (adj.) | *sneaky* | Page | 25 |

| **garrulous** | (adj.) | *talkative* | Page | 47 |
| loquacious | | | | |
| prolix | | | | |
| verbose | | | | |
| voluble | | | | |

| **germane** | (adj.) | *appropriate* | Page | 3 |
| apposite | | | | |
| apropos | | | | |
| pertinent | | | | |
| relevant | | | | |

| **halcyon** | (adj.) | *calm* | Page | 36 |
| concordant | | | | |
| pacific | | | | |
| serene | | | | |
| tranquil | | | | |

| **heinous** | (adj.) | *hateful* | Page | 36 |
| base | | | | |
| iniquitous | | | | |
| nefarious | | | | |
| vile | | | | |

| **hone** | (v.) | *to sharpen* | Page | 48 |
| edge | | | | |
| whet | | | | |

| **horde** | (n.) | *a crowd* | Page | 14 |
| deluge | | | | |
| galaxy | | | | |
| legion | | | | |
| panoply | | | | |
| spate | | | | |
| swarm | | | | |

| **hyperbole** | (n.) | *exaggeration* | Page | 48 |
| amplification | | | | |
| overstatement | | | | |
| superlative | | | | |

| **imbibe** | (v.) | *to drink* | Page | 14 |
| guzzle | | | | |
| quaff | | | | |

| **imperial** | (adj.) | *majestic* | Page | 25 |
| monarchal | | | | |
| regal | | | | |
| sovereign | | | | |

| **impromptu** | (adj.) | *unplanned* | Page | 36 |
| extemporaneous | | | | |
| improvised | | | | |
| spontaneous | | | | |

| **inception** | (n.) | *a beginning* | Page | 36 |
| genesis | | | | |
| inchoation | | | | |
| incipience | | | | |

| **incorrigible** | (adj.) | *hopeless, beyond control* | Page | 14 |
| confirmed | | | | |
| intractable | | | | |
| irreparable | | | | |
| refractory | | | | |

| **indelible** | (adj.) | *permanent* | Page | 3 |
| immutable | | | | |
| irreparable | | | | |
| irrevocable | | | | |

| **inebriate** | (v.) | *to make drunk* | Page | 48 |
| besot | | | | |
| intoxicate | | | | |

| **inter** | (v.) | *to bury* | Page | 15 |
| entomb | | | | |
| inhume | | | | |
| sepulture | | | | |

| **lascivious** | (adj.) | *lustful* | Page | 15 |
| lecherous | | | | |
| lewd | | | | |
| obscene | | | | |

| **libertine** | (n.) | *womanizer* | Page | 15 |
| lecher | | | | |
| philanderer | | | | |
| seducer | | | | |

| **lithe** | (adj.) | *graceful, bending easily* | Page | 15 |
| agile | | | | |
| supple | | | | |
| willowy | | | | |

| **lode** | (n.) | *rich source, gold mine* | Page | 25 |
| fount | | | | |
| quarry | | | | |
| staple | | | | |

**repartée** (n.) *witticism* Page 26
   levity
   pleasantry
   quip
   retort

**reverberate** (v.) *to echo* Page 27
   rebound
   resonate
   resound

**ribald** (adj.) *vulgar* Page 4
   coarse
   irreverent
   obscene
   scurrilous

**salacious** (adj.) *lustful* Page 49
   carnal
   lascivious
   lecherous
   lewd

**sanction** (n.) *law* Page 16
   decree
   countenance (v.) *to consent*
   esteem
   ratify

**servile** (adj.) *slavish* Page 27
   deferential
   fawning
   obsequious

**shyster** (n.) *swindler* Page 4
   defrauder
   quack
   trickster

**sparse** (adj.) *scarce* Page 38
   exiguous
   meager
   scant

**spurious** (adj.) *counterfeit* Page 5
   ersatz
   simulated
   supposititious

# POWERWORDS™
# SAT® VERBAL PREP SERIES

## PowerWords™ SAT® Verbal Prep Vocabulary Workbooks

Workbook 1
Workbook 2
Workbook 3

## PowerWords™ SAT® Verbal Prep Cartoon Flashcards

Set 1
Set 2
Set 3

## PowerWords™ SAT® Verbal Prep Audio Cassette

### Rhythm, Rhyme & Rap
*(Includes Vocabulary Cartoon Booklet)*

# POWERWORDS ™

## SAT®
## VERBAL PREP WORKBOOK
# LEARN IT
# FOR THE
# SAT–
# USE IT
# FOR LIFE

ISBN# 1-879871-07-6

ISBN 1-879871-07-6

90000 >

EAN

9 781879 871076